S0-AZQ-628

J 782.4216 BOD
Bodden, Valerie,
One Direction /
STMR

STMR
APR 2015

THE
BIG
TIME

ONE DIRECTION

VALERIE BODDEN

Tulare County Library

ONE DIRECTION

TABLE OF CONTENTS

MEET ONE DIRECTION

Thousands of young fans crowd a dark *arena*. They watch a video of five boys at the beach. Suddenly, the video ends. The boys are on the stage. They start singing. The fans scream. They love One Direction!

One Direction is a boy band. It was formed in 2010. The band has five members: Niall Horan, Zayn Malik, Liam Payne, Harry Styles, and Louis Tomlinson.

Niall, Louis, Zayn, Liam (opposite), and Harry (right) like to sing pop music.

ONE DIRECTION'S CHILDHOODS

Louis is the oldest member of One Direction. He was born in 1991. Niall, Zayn, and Liam were all born in 1993. Harry was born in 1994. Louis, Zayn, Harry, and Liam are from England. Niall is from Ireland.

One Direction has fans all around the world.

IRELAND

ENGLAND

GETTING INTO MUSIC

The members of One Direction did not know each other when they were young. But they each liked to sing. Louis and Zayn were both in *musicals*. Harry started a band. Niall was in talent shows. Liam studied *music technology* in college.

Zayn grew up with his parents, one older sister, and two younger sisters.

In 2010, Louis, Zayn, Harry, Niall, and Liam tried out for the TV singing contest *The X Factor*. None of them made it very far on their own. But the show's judges said the boys should form a group. They became One Direction.

Judge Simon Cowell helped One Direction become a famous boy band.

THE BIG TIME

One Direction took third place in *The X Factor*. Afterward, *X Factor* judge Simon Cowell gave them a recording *contract*. One Direction's first album, *Up All Night*, came out in 2011.

The boys were excited to see their pictures on magazines, posters, and TV.

Their next album, *Take Me Home*, came out in 2012. One Direction went on tour, too. They performed in cities around the world. One Direction has won a **BRIT Award** and many MTV awards.

Fans who love listening to One Direction's music are called "Directioners."

OFF THE STAGE

When they are not singing, the boys of One Direction like to have fun. They play pranks on each other. They play video games and soccer together.

In 2013, Liam went surfing in Australia (left).

WHAT IS NEXT?

One Direction planned to make a new album every year or so. Some of the band members said they might try acting, too. With so much going on, One Direction is likely to keep fans excited for many years!

The boys take turns singing during hit songs like "Story of My Life."

WHAT ONE DIRECTION SAYS ABOUT …

BEING YOURSELF

"Things change, people change, but you will always be you, so stay true to yourself." –Zayn

DREAMS COMING TRUE

"Even though I'd always wanted to be in a band …, I never imagined it would actually happen." –Harry

FORMING A BAND

"My first thought was, 'Are we going to make this work when we don't know each other?' It was such a leap of faith." –Liam

GLOSSARY

arena a large building with many seats that holds sports events or concerts

BRIT Award one of the biggest music awards in England

contract an agreement between two people or groups

music technology the use of computers to help make music

musicals plays in which the characters sing a lot

READ MORE

Lüsted, Marcia Amidon. *One Direction: Breakout Boy Band*. Minneapolis: Lerner, 2013.

Salazar, Sam. *One Direction*. New York: Gareth Stevens, 2014.

Tieck, Sarah. *One Direction*. Minneapolis: Abdo, 2013.

WEBSITES

One Direction
http://www.onedirectionmusic.com/us/home/
This is the band's own site, with pictures, videos, and more.

One Direction.com
http://www.onedirection.com/
This One Direction fan site has lots of information on what the band is up to.

INDEX

PUBLISHED BY Creative Education
P.O. Box 227, Mankato, Minnesota 56002
Creative Education is an imprint of The Creative Company
www.thecreativecompany.us

DESIGN AND PRODUCTION BY Christine Vanderbeek
PRINTED IN the United States of America

PHOTOGRAPHS BY Alamy (Everett Collection Inc, London Entertainment), Corbis (MARIO ANZUONI/Reuters, Roger Bentley/Splash News, R Chiang/Splash News, Deano/Splash News, sergione infuso/Demotix, KirBan/Grey Wasp/Splash News, Christopher Peterson/Splash News, Splash News/Splash News), iStockphoto (colevineyard), Shutterstock (ekler, Featureflash, JStone, Mr Pics)

COPYRIGHT © 2015 CREATIVE EDUCATION
International copyright reserved in all countries. No part of this book may be reproduced in any form without written permission from the publisher.

LIBRARY OF CONGRESS CATALOGING-IN-PUBLICATION DATA
Bodden, Valerie.
One Direction / Valerie Bodden.
p. cm. — (The big time)
Includes index.
Summary: An elementary introduction to the lives, work, and popularity of One Direction, a British pop group formed on the TV singing contest *The X Factor* known for such songs as "What Makes You Beautiful."

ISBN 978-1-60818-497-2
1. One Direction (Musical group)—Juvenile literature. 2. Rock musicians—England—Biography—Juvenile literature. I. Title.
ML3930.O66B64 2015
782.42164092'2—dc23 [B]   2014000251

CCSS: RI.1.1, 2, 3, 4, 5, 6, 7; RI.2.1, 2, 5, 6, 7; RI.3.1, 5, 7, 8; RI.4.3, 5; RF.1.1, 3, 4; RF.2.3, 4

FIRST EDITION
9 8 7 6 5 4 3 2 1

Note: Every effort has been made to ensure that the websites listed above are suitable for children, that they have educational value, and that they contain no inappropriate material. However, because of the nature of the Internet, it is impossible to guarantee that these sites will remain active indefinitely or that their contents will not be altered.